T0354968

MUSINGS
OF A
PRIVATE
MAN

MUSINGS
OF A
PRIVATE
MAN

WILLIAM A. HORSTMAN

MUSINGS OF A PRIVATE MAN

iUniverse books may be ordered through booksellers or by contacting:

iUniverse
1663 Liberty Drive
Bloomington, IN 47403
www.iuniverse.com
844-349-9409

ISBN: 978-1-6632-6862-4 (sc)
ISBN: 978-1-6632-6861-7 (e)

Print information available on the last page.

iUniverse rev. date: 01/28/2025

CONTENTS

PROLOGUE

I only knew Bill Horstman for the last phase of his life, living across the alley from me with his beloved Sally and their dog Fig. A true gentle man, he was witty, and thoughtful; a man who was never too much or too little. When I'd see him in the neighborhood, mostly walking his dog Fig, he often reminded me that he, too, had a redheaded child. My daughter's hair is quite red and seeing her occasionally seemed to bring Bill closer to his past. Once when I ran into him on the sidewalk, he showed me a picture of his son with red hair, he told me that he had been carrying the picture around in case he ran into me. Bill always seemed familiar to me - from the same part of the Midwest, we ended up on the same block. Taking a just left of center stance on most things, he had the same way of speaking and the mannerisms I knew so well. I spent a lot of time in the neighborhoods he grew up in - Shorewood in Milwaukee, Plymouth just north of there, and then further north where his family's ancestral home was on the Baraboo River, North Freedom, Wisconsin. Bill's Dad was from Indiana, and he went to Purdue, just like my dad had. But his dad was a craftsman and did woodwork in the basement, including making a fly fishing rod. His dad taught Bill how to fish. Then Bill's dad died of a heart attack in their North Freedom home on November 24, 1951 when Bill was 9 years old. Bill wrote about him in 'Fly fishing rod,' and the final line of that story, "late in November in Wisconsin and the trout have gone deep and still in their pools," is one of the most beautiful lines I have come across.

For a year or so I was in a small writing group with Bill. We met monthly, shared whatever pieces we were working on, and gave kind feedback. Early on Bill would stand up and read aloud his poems and short stories. They were beautiful, brief, funny, and touching. Some were about his past, his family growing up, or his first marriage, his kids, but many about his present, his partner Sally and their dog Fig, and a few about the current state of affairs. Really, they are some of the best kinds of life commentary. Bill was the speech writer for the Chancellor at the University of Wisconsin, Milwaukee (UWM) for many years, so he had that style of being behind the scenes, the astute observer, needing no accolades, no fame. In fact, standing up at an open mic and reading his short stories to an audience seems like a remarkable feat for such a quiet man, but maybe he came to it later in his life, maybe it was his time for his words.

The most important thing I learned about Bill was his experience with Carl Sagan's book *Contact*. There is a story in this collection that Bill wrote called *Contact*. It's not a finished piece, nor is it a very cohesive piece, but the experience he is trying to capture is one of the most fascinating and extraordinary events I have ever heard of, and it's something I will never forget. As you'll read, when Bill was about 30 years old, he was on a flight home from California, and he had the book *Contact* that he began reading on that flight. Early in the book a few things jump out to Bill. First, the location of the novel begins in a Wisconsin town near a lake, just like how Bill had grown up near Lake Michigan. Then we find out the main character has lost her father while she's in grade school, in a sudden way, just as Bill had. But to confirm that this book, which Carl Sagan wrote in 1985, was indeed connected to Bill, was the passage that read his exact name. The sentence is: *Billy Horstman, who sat next to her, gently reached out and placed his hand over hers.*

Astounding.

When Bill told our small writing group this series of events, over 30 years after they had happened, he was calm but had a lingering perplexity. He told us that when he had read the passage with his name he "felt a zipper open in the sky," and he "saw... another world?' He wasn't sure. Bill began to have questions about time, like Carl Sagan did, and like Ellie, the main character in the novel, did. Is it possible to travel backwards in time? Is time linear? Are there various layers of time? And various existences along those layers?

For those who read the book *Contact*, or saw the 1997 film, the story is ostensibly about making contact with extraterrestrials, but in fact it's about Ellie's longing for her father. You'll find in Bill's writing this same longing. So, my thought was: is this the contact that was being made? It seemed that Ellie and Bill had a connection, an empathic reassurance was passed from Billy to Ellie when he comforted her in class, and they certainly shared an understanding. So, as Ellie was attempting to make contact with her father, could it be that Bill's father was making contact with him, through Carl Sagan?

But how does something like this happen?

In the novel Sagan's narrative explores the profound implications of discovering intelligent extraterrestrial life. It delves into the complexities and challenges humanity might face in such an encounter, including terrorism, government interference, and personal sacrifices. Despite these obstacles, the novel maintains an optimistic outlook, portraying the universe as a potentially welcoming place where humanity is not alone. However, at the end Ellie discovers proof of the existence of God. This revelation contrasts with the scientific and rational exploration of alien intelligence throughout the rest of the novel. It adds a spiritual dimension to the story, challenging both the characters and the readers to consider the intersection of science and faith. Was it this twist that Bill needed to confront? I imagine he was living a purely scientific exploration of life, again one familiar to my upbringing - a paradigm without religion that hardly recognized time travel or alien existence, let alone communication with the dead. Yet this intersection of science and spirituality and mortality may be exactly what Bill needed. And yet, it doesn't seem as if Bill ever reconciled this for himself or gained much satisfaction in its pursuit.

Later, Sagan said this about his book,

> As I imagine it, there will be a multilayered message. First there is a beacon, an announcement signal, something that says, Pay attention. This is not some natural astronomical phenomenon. This is a signal from intelligent beings … Then, the next layer is one that says, This message is directed specifically to you guys on Earth. It isn't directed to anybody else. And the third part of the message is the real content, which is a very complex set of data in a new language, which is also explained.

I have to believe that was Bill's moment, on the plane, when a beacon announced, Pay Attention! Bill told us at that moment when he read himself in Sagan's book, "It was as if there was a before and an after." But did he decipher the 'real content' that Sagan speaks of, 'the very complex set of data'? I can't say.

It turns out this was Carl Sagan's specialty, an exploration of direct communication, across planes of time and life forms. Not only is it that when we read a book, we can have the experience that an author is speaking directly to us, sharing their insights, stories, and perspectives, which transcend barriers of distance and time, but that an author can channel information that arrived to them from the cosmos and unknowingly send it back out to someone through a book. Sagan discusses this in his *Cosmos* talks:

> *What an astonishing thing a book is. It's a flat object made from a tree with flexible parts on which are imprinted lots of funny dark squiggles. But one glance at it and you're inside the mind of another person, maybe somebody dead for thousands of years. Across the millennia, an author is speaking clearly and silently inside your head, directly to you. Writing is perhaps the greatest of human inventions, binding together people who never knew each other, citizens of distant epochs. Books break the shackles of time. A book is proof that humans are capable of working magic.*

Towards the end of our time together, when Bill's brain was just starting to fail him but before Covid arrived and our group disbanded, Bill was a hit or miss for group meetings. I knew he badly wanted to be there. A few times I picked him up to give him rides, a few times Sally helped him find his way, but for one group he left his house and never showed up at our meeting. The final meeting we had with Bill he had nearly lost his voice, but his eyes were smiling, and he read one of his short stories - one he had read several times to us, always making the same comments and critiques about his own work, all of which were a treasure to take in. But he was fading.

In the book *Contact*, there's a gesture that would be easy to overlook as it is subtle and only briefly mentioned, but gestures are fundamental ways human transmit ideas, and this one, this tender, non-intrusive offering of a true connection in it's effortless physicality, seems in the particular style of the Bill who I knew:

> *Billy Horstman, who sat next to her, gently reached out and placed his hand over hers.*

Much later, after Bill tragically passed, his widow Sally found me in the alley one early morning when she was walking Fig. She had taken over dog walking duty since he had gone. Sally said to me, "I have his writings," and I knew exactly what she meant. I also knew how significant it was that she was sharing this with me. Later that day I was in Bill's office in their home. I saw where Bill sat at his computer, and also where he sat with her most nights in their beautiful home that they had created together. That afternoon Sally and I gathered all of his papers in file folders and also a flash drive of the digital copies, and as I walked with this load back across the alley, I knew I had a treasure in my arms. Then, over the series of many months, and with the invaluable help of the author Barbara Monier, we carefully arranged Bill's writings, which follow here in alphabetical order. My hope is that it can be a treasure for anyone else who has the time and interest in these thoughtful, poignant pieces by Bill Horstman, for maybe he is channeling a message for someone out there.

Brooke Laufer

70 \ 71

I recently finished living 70 years. When asked my age, I say "I'm 70." But I'm 70 only by a trick of the calendar. On my 70th birthday, I was beginning my 71st year. My 70th year of life was behind me. I was no longer 70.

I (and you, too) have lived a year longer than our celebrated birthday age because we didn't get years-credit for existing until we had completed 12 months post-partum. We had a birth day and then 12 months later we had our first birthday. Until we had lived for an entire year, we were zero years old. Zero! In the same way, until I had lived for 70 years, I was not 70 years old but rather 69 years and <364 days old. This way of counting years by the CURRENT year, not the one you just finished living (the ELAPSED year), is a product of the Gregorian calendar in which there is no zero.

Remember the kafuffle when the current millennium began? Most people celebrated the new millennium when 1999 changed to 2000; but a minority celebrated when the 2000th year was over. They began counting the new millennium on January 1, 2001. In a 1999 episode of the television series The X Files, Dana Scully explains to her partner, Fox Mulder, the elapsed year way of counting and says she will celebrate the new millennium at the start of 2001. Mulder replies, "Nobody likes a math geek, Scully."

To me, this distinction is only important because although I say "I'm 70," I'm EVEN OLDER THAN THAT. Why is that? What's so bad about being 70/1?

Well, for starters, it's a deeply embedded bias in our culture. As the writer Steve Rushin recently wrote: "Seventy is a milestone, the biblical age of threescore and 10, when a man has, in Mark Twain's words, reached his 'scriptural statute of limitations.' The Yankees fired Casey Stengel as their manager at that age. "I'll never make the mistake of being 70 again,' Stengel said."

It's often said now that "70 is the new "50." This is said about 70-year-olds who have inherited hardy genes, have most of their hair and original teeth, have been spared devastating cases of cancer, Parkinson's, heart attack, stroke or organ failure; who don't smoke or drink heavily, who take a daily multi-vitamin, who walk briskly, and who have really, really, really good health insurance. For these people, 70 is like their parents' 50. For the other 70 year olds, 70 is like their parents' 70.

My parents and the others of their generation lived in a pre-tofu world. The life practices that would hasten their death (meat & butter, cigarettes, alcohol, obesity, lack of exercise) were not yet seen as contributors to poor health. And the advanced knowledge and treatments that now prolong life - regular health screening, cholesterol-lowering drugs, antibiotics, vaccines, early cancer diagnosis and treatment - were not part of their lives.

Even though I am one of the fortunate ones, one of the "new 70s," here's the kicker about 70/1: Our culture now sees me as officially old. If someone who knows my age says to me "You look good," the sentence now is completed by the phrase, "for your age."

Seventy years old is a perceptual key in our culture. In most people's view, I have unlocked and passed through the doorway between middle age and old age. The writer and editor Malcolm Cowley in his essay "The View From 80" writes, "We start by growing old in other people's eyes, then slowly we come to share their judgment."

I don't as yet share that judgment although I know well how many years (70? 71?) I've accumulated and the toll those years have extracted. But I don't want to be typed, and mostly I don't want to see myself through the lens of age. As a number, age is an abstraction, a human creation, not a category of being.

Old age bias inhabits the same kind of exclusionary room that children are put in, just on the other end of the age spectrum: *Infants* advance to *children*, then to *adolescents* or *teenagers* before being recognized as *adults*. Each stage has its *expectations, rewards, and punishments.*

For example, I vividly remember the first time I was addressed by a store clerk as "sir." I was 17. I was looking at sport coats in a Milwaukee men's clothing store. The clerk approached me and said, "May I help you, sir?"

Not *young man* or *young fella* but "SIR." I knew instantly that I had arrived in a new and better cultural room. In the public eye, I had gone through the doorway to the *adult room.*

For the 70/71 and older crowd, our culture has a different set of expectations, rewards, and punishments.

Expectations: Don't chase fashion either in attire or language; clothes and jargon do not make the man or woman. Don't wear a Speedo; it shows the ravages of time more than the good parts you have left. Don't go on and on about age-related physical and mental problems. Everyone has them and it's boring. In short, don't run from your age. Stop and give it a hug.

Rewards: More kindly treatment; People you pass on the street are likely to smile back and to let you pet their dog. Social Security & Medicare; More time for passions/interests, people, pets, beauty, acceptance, failure. My friend Terry suggests that I embrace my advanced age by creating a *Fuck It List*. On this list would be all the things I've grudgingly tolerated but now don't have to give a damn about. Freed from the noose of my wants, and fears, and prejudices, 70/71 and alive is pretty damn good.

The great boxing champ Joe Lewis was unbeatable in the 1930's and 1940's. By the 1950's he was very vulnerable. When asked how he kept boxing when his skills were much diminished, Lewis said, "I did the best I could with what I had. Got to go with what you got."

Punishments: Pain. Physical stuff that goes wrong doesn't get "fixed. It only improves. Sense of accelerated time and of one's own mortality. Frequent, steady loss of beloved people and creatures. For me, that's the worst loss.

Now our culture has nudged me though a different doorway. Out of the *adult* or *middle age* room into the *old people's* room. I can't control what other people think, but I do have some control over my self-perception. I can try to live without regard to our culture's ageist expectations. To paraphrase Joe Lewis, I can do my best to go with what I've got.

September 2019

20 DEFINITIONS

1. ARBITRATOR: A cook who leaves Arby's to work at McDonalds

2. AVOIDABLE: What a bullfighter tries to do

3. BERNADETTE: The act of torching a mortgage

4. BURGLARIZE: What a crook sees with

5. CONTROL: Fooling a short, ugly guy

6. COUNTERFEITERS: Workers who put together kitchen cabinets

7. ECLIPSE: What an English barber does for a living

8. EYEDROPPER: A clumsy ophthalmologist

9. HEROES: What a guy in a boat does

10. LEFTBANK: What the robber did when his bag was full of money

11. MISTY: How golfers create divots

12. PARADOX: Two physicians

13. PARASITES: What you see from the top of the Eiffel Tower

14. PHARMACIST: A helper on the farm

15. POLARIZE: What penguins see with

16. PRIMATE: Forcibly removing your spouse from in front of the TV

17. RELIEF: What trees do in the spring

18. RUBBERNECK: What you do to relax your wife

19. SELFISH: What the owner of a seafood store does

20. SUDAFED: Brought litigation against a government official!

A LITTLE SPRING SONG FOR YOU

Spring's finally showing her face,
but modestly

Sunlight through my window
is strong and early
but freezing air's only
a transparent pane away.

Today, I'm going to believe
in the sunlight.

(Received April 5, 2013)

A PUN ON PORPOISE

A marine biologist developed a species of genetically engineered dolphins that could live forever if they were fed a steady diet of seagulls.

One day his supply of the birds ran out, so he had to go out and trap some more. On the way back, he spied two lions asleep on the road. Afraid to wake them, he gingerly stepped over them.

Immediately, he was arrested and charged with transporting gulls across sedate lions for immortal porpoises.

A STORY OF EASTERN EUROPEAN CONFUSION AND HUNGRY BEARS

While visiting Yellowstone Park, two Eastern Europeans happen on a family of bears.

The Czech runs up to the bears and, while trying to photograph the momma bear, is mauled and eaten.

The Pole runs to the nearest park ranger and says: A bear just ate my friend!

The Pole and the ranger run to find the bears, and the Pole mistakenly points to the papa bear and says: "That's the one that ate my friend."

The park ranger shoots the papa bear, but they don't find his friend inside. The ranger then shoots the momma bear, and they find the remains of the Pole's friend inside the momma bear.

The moral of this story is:

Never trust a Pole who says the Czech is in the male.

ALL YOUR ROOMS

If I were free to visit
all the rooms of your house

to wander from study to
bedroom to sun filled porch

and smell your lilac hair
all ways and everywhere

I would then leave
your rooms untouched

and wait a summons
outside your unwatched walls

knowing that your honeyed tea
awaited me

AS I WALK PAST

my childhood home

phantom elm trees
overarch our yard

crickets sing
their ancestral song

other parents light
my family's porch

as I gather ghosts
in the near night

April 2020

AUSSIE SKIT

Narrator (N):

Ladies and Gentlemen! The Friendship Forces of Chicago and Northern Illinois are pleased to present the drama

Waiting for the Adelaidians

Tonight's world premier presentation has been produced in cooperation with

Unrehearsed Studios,
Unpublished Writers Guild, and
Cheap Props Incorporated

The city: Chicago, Illinois, U.S.A.

The time: 2015

The scene:

It's night *(turn off flashlight)*. And it's cold *(dump ice cubes)* and windy *(turn on hairdryer)*.

As the curtain rises, *(roll up towel attached a dowel)*, President Barack Obama and First Lady Michelle Obama are in their Chicago home talking about the upcoming visit of people from Adelaide, Australia to Chicago. Let's listen in.

Michelle Obama (**MO**): "Barack, I need your help for a few minutes".

Barack Obama (**BO**): "I'm way ahead of you there, sweetheart. I took the garbage out 2 hours ago."

MO: "That's nice, babe, but this is something else. The Friendship Force groups from Chicago and Northern Illinois asked us to help plan a visit from the Adelaide, Australia Friendship Force. You know, give them some ideas that we, as long-time Chicagoans, think are interesting and representative of our city."

BO: "I'd really like to help out, but I'm pretty busy just now – saving the environment, keeping the economy going, promoting world peace. Plus, I promised Sasha I'd I help with her algebra homework tonight."

MO: "Barack! If you had time to play basketball this afternoon, you can spare a few minutes to help me out here. Besides, I already agreed that we'd do this."

BO: "Okay, okay. Let's start with the Chicagoan who these Australians know best. That person might know what our visitors are like & what Chicago has that will interest them. Do we know the Chicagoan who people from Adelaide know best? I hope it's not Rod Blagojevich."

MO: "No, it's not Blago. But you won't like the real answer any better. A recent survey shows that when our visitors think of Chicago, the first person they think of is ... Al Capone. And the group of people they think of first is ... gangsters."

BO: "Well, Al and his gang have been dead for years. Fortunately, my Presidential Super Secret Service developed this mobile phone *(shows unconnected rotary dial phone)* that allows me to communicate across time and space."

MO: "Oh, I LOVE that App!"

BO: "I'll just dial C- A- P- O- N- E." *(dials)*

AL CAPONE (AC): *(Shakes wooden cow bell to simulate phone ringing & then uses bell as his phone)* "Yeah, Capone here. Whadda ya want?"

BO: Mr. Capone, this is President Barack Obama. I'm trying to get ideas about what people from Australia would like to see in Chicago. They seem to know about you, so I thought you might know about them.

AC: "President Obama? I thought Herbert Hoover was President. Ahh, never mind, I'm a little behind on the news, being dead and all. Tell ya, Barack, I don't know nothin' about Australia first hand. But my gang hears a lot of stuff on the street. May or may not be true, but lemme me ask 'em (*consults quickly with gang members*). Okay, here's what they've heard about Australians."

GANG MEMBERS (GM): (*They take turns saying one "fact"*)

"Kangaroos are the main form of public transportation
Everyone lives on the beach and rides surfboards
Australians only eat barbeque, Vegemite, and Tim Tams
They drink a lot of beer
They wrestle salt-water crocodiles
Instead of dogs and cats for pets, they have Emus, Dingoes, Koalas, and Kookaburras
Most of their continent is a desert.
They all drive Subaru Outbacks
Some early English settlers were prisoners."

MO: "Barack, those sound mostly like stereotypes. They only things that might be useful, if they're true, are "drinking beer" because Chicagoans like beer a lot, too. And the prisoner settlements - which we can relate to because most of our Illinois Governors get sent to prison."

GM: (*Intone together*) "Otto Kerner, Dan Walker, George Ryan, Rod Blagojevich" (*Bla-go-je-vich sung with harmonic gusto*)

BO: "You're right, Michelle. Al and his gang don't have much real information about Australia. But ... you mentioned earlier that the Adelaide visitors were surveyed about what they associate with the word "Chicago." What's on that survey besides Al Capone and gangsters?"

MO: (*Michelle briefly consults with the gangsters*) "Here are the results from the things or people most often to the least often associated with Chicago."

GM: (*They take turns saying one item*)

"Windy
Architecture
Sky Scrapers
Music
Millennium Park
Great Lakes
Snow & Cold
Frank Lloyd Wright
Cars
Movies
Hot Dogs
Cattle Yards
… and *(in harmonic unison)* "OBAMA"

BO: "I was last!? Maybe I'd get more recognition if I were a "windier" politician — like that funny haired, real estate guy who plastered his name on one of our skyscrapers. You know, whatshisname - "Dump…Bunk…Trunk?" Oh, well."

"Does that list help, Michelle?"

MO: "Yes, Barack. I think our Friendship Force groups can work up an interesting itinerary from that list. And they'll get to know the real, not the stereotypical, Australians at the same time. Friendship Force: What a great organization! Sounds like they're working with you on promoting World Peace, Barack."

NARRATOR: And so, the curtain closes *(unroll towel)* and the lights go up *(turn on flashlight)* on this Chicago drama. But before the mists of time *(use spray bottle)* close over the scene, here's a little song from all of us to all of you. (With apologies to Frank Sinatra, Sammy Cahn, and Jimmy van Heusen):

(Characters join arms and sing a modified version of "My Kind of Town")

"Now this could only happen to guys like you
       And only happen in a town like this

So may we say to each of you most gratef'lly
        As we throw each one of you a kiss

(*All throw a kiss*)

This is your kind of town, Chicago is
        Your kind of town, Chicago is
Your kind of people too
        People who smile at you

(*Slow tempo for big finish*)

And each time you roam, Chicago is
        Your second home, Chicago is

(*Leg kicks*)

One town that won't let you down
        It's your kind of town"

Notes:

    The Characters:

        Al Capone, Barack Obama, Michelle Obama,
        Narrator, six Gangsters

    Cheap Props:

        Fedoras, rotary phone, sunglasses, hairdryer,
        flashlight, rolled-up towel, ice cube tray & bucket,
        wood bell/phone, spray bottle

- First version 2015
- Final version 2020

BREAKING NEWS

Congressman Anthony Weiner just announced he will run for President, and he has selected Attorney General Eric Holder as his Vice-Presidential running mate.

WEINER-HOLDER IN 2012!

(You just knew that something like this would happen.)

BROTHERS ACT

...while we're talking about "rage," I want to comment on a highway behavior that may trigger this more than any other. This is the person who drives in the left lane at the same speed as the person in the right lane. And they drive slowly, which is to say the speed limit. We used to call this a "brothers' act" – like two ditzy Siamese twin brothers joined right hip to left hip, rolling through your life at the same pace.

I used to think that this happened mostly by accident. Some person of diminished capacity (your elderly aunt Gladys, a guy from Nebraska, a person talking with his passenger, someone who lacks the strength in their right foot to push the accelerator any further, a guy having a stroke). And that was irritating enough. You want to pass the guy in the right lane. And so do the 14 cars right behind you about 2 feet apart, seething with anger and shouting to no-one who can hear "pull over, goddamnit, you idiot!!"

But I recently found out (though reliable sources who I am not at liberty to reveal) that this is **never** just an accident. The person in the left lane is **always** doing this intentionally.

These people, and there are thousands of them worldwide, and they are all members of a secret society devoted only to doing this. They are all named Mary. Or Walter. They are all former nuns or priests in Opus Dei. Who were expelled for being too strict.

They were part of a teaching order, and when children misbehaved, instead of rapping their knuckles with a ruler, they would use a meat cleaver.

So they were expelled from Opus Dei. And given old cars to drive. Don't ask me why. They just were. This is a conspiracy theory remember. You just have to take some things on faith.

The Marys and the Walters get directions every morning, right after their self-flagellation, about where YOU are going to be driving. They drive ahead of you until they find a car in the right lane going really slow (that is to say, the speed limit). They wait until you are in their driver's side mirror and they pull into the left lane. And stay there.

Mary and Walter have an inflamed sense of ethics when it comes to obeying driving laws. They are like an interstate highway Moseses bringing speed limits, and don't pass, and slow for tractors, and don't fornicate in the front seat on curves on stone tablets from their weird little brains to impose on you. They are self-designated road-Nazis.

And now that we know this about them, I think that a little vigilante justice is required to keep our highways safe for excessive speeding – which is our right in America. It's implied somewhere in the Bill of Rights. I think.

Anyway, it's our civic duty to run Mary's and Walter's cars into large roadside trees. (Pause). I know some of you may be thinking, "Isn't that a little excessive? Running Mary off the road into a tree? Like, what has that tree done to deserve being hit by a car going the speed limit?"

You're right. The tree is innocent. But think of the alternatives – if you run Walter into an electrical tower, people for miles around would be without TV for a couple of hours. Think of that: young children with no smack-down wrestling. Morons with no Bill O'Reilly. For hours.

Or if you run Mary into an oncoming lane of traffic, there's always the chance that there might be someone nice in that car – someone who might have bought you a beer one day. Or slept with you. Or maybe a puppy who would grow up to be Lassie and who would rescue one of your kids who fell down an old well. Although you warned Timmy not to play near the McCoy's abandoned farm.

On the other hand, it might be one of my ex-wives. (Pause & consider.) But, no, we don't want to think about that. We're not barbarians here. We just want to do some "highway cleansing." Just kill Mary and Walter. To make America Safe for Speeding. (softly sing a stanza of "Proud to be an American" & end).

COMEDY

Comedy "crouches"

First public exposure. Anxiety about mentioning this – unlike family & friends who are basically paid to be considerate (because you can always get back at them), with people you don't know, showing vulnerability is more like bloodletting in front of a school of sharks. Inviting problems.

And unlike when people pay to see a known comedian, you have nothing invested in laughing. If you pay to see Jerry Seinfeld (or Larry the Cable Guy) you are personally committed to thinking he's funny – even if would just stand there, people would probably laugh. They've already paid money to laugh.

Look at the audience on the TV comedy shows – a comic comes on stage and people already have these big grins – they can hardly wait to laugh and to be seen laughing so that everybody watching knows they got their money's worth. But here, it's different. You have no reason to want me to be amusing. You may even have come here hoping to see me fail. Well, shame on you! I'm very disappointed. And so are your parents.

And this brings me to heckling. Which is another fear. Not just someone who's drunk or stupidly belligerent, but someone who gets off a clever crack at your expense. I guess the challenge then is to retort this person with an equally clever put-down – something better that "I know you are but what am I?" Or at least not get visibly rattled.

My problem here is that I was brought up 50 years ago in this middle class second generation German household where the public ethic was always to "make nice." No matter what you were doing to someone – shooting them, divorcing them, shredding their self esteem in some horrible Lutheran-guilt-shame way, it was always done in an indirect way. You never just confronted someone & got in their face. So if someone heckles me, my first reaction is to smile and shrug and silently wonder why their mother didn't teach them better manners.

But I realize that this is a different time and anyone who comes up here is fair game.

I also think it's fair to note that it probably isn't as safe to be a heckler as it once was. Just like driving. You used to be able to yell out the window or flip a finger to someone and usually they'd just respond the same way. Or maybe you'd get into a fist fight. But this is the age of road rage. You scowl at the wrong person and you're dodging bullets or getting run off the road.

Well it's the same driving crowd that's at today's public events. And on the stages. The next guy you heckle may be seized by "stage rage" and really flip on you. "Hey, you're NOT Funny!" "You sonofabitch! That's the last time you'll talk to me like that. Pulls a water pistol. Composes self. Not that I would ever do that. Remember, I was trained to make nice. No rage built up here. Twitch.

COMEDY GRADUATION SPEECH

Bill Horstman
Comedy College 202 (final)
Graduation Class Routine
The Cubby Bear (Chicago)
March 12, 2008

Hi. I'm Bill Horstman. You may have heard my name in the news recently. I'm the guy who isn't fucking Sarah Silverman. Or Matt Damon, Jimmy Kimmel, or Ben Affleck. Or anyone they're fucking.

Not that anyone thought I was, but it was an opportunity to say, "fuck" three times just introducing myself. We're taught in Comedy College that we have to say "fuck" a lot in stand-up. Going for an "A" in this class. Give it up for our Comedy College instructor, Jim Rauth. He takes money from grown people to teach them how to swear and tell lies in public effectively. Gee, your parents must be proud, Jim.

I've been following the Presidential primary races pretty closely. Not the main steam media. Delegate counts. Vote totals. Boring! I follow the kind of news you get at the Jewel checkout line. In The Star, Sun, National Enquirer. News you give a shit about. Who's the love child of Marilyn and Martin Luther King? One guess on that one. Which candidates were hatched from alien genes in area 51? Turns out, only Dennis Kucinich. I would have guessed most of them. So, here's some campaign, News Behind the News:

Where are they now? Candidates who have dropped out. Mitt Romney. His full first name is "Mittens." Named after the family cat. Played together as a kid in the litter box. Learned how to bury his shit. Good lesson for a politician. Too bad Eliot Spitzer didn't talk more with Mittens about this. John Edwards. Running for office again in North Carolina. Getting a bad haircut and his teeth un-straightened to appeal to the cracker asshole constituency. Fred Thompson. He of the well-lined face and baggy jowls. Being investigated for mob ties. FBI got a search warrant for his jowls and discovered Jimmy Hoffa's body buried under them. That Baptist guy –Huckleberry. He doesn't have a job. So he' going to stay on the road - a little picking and strumming, a little Mayberry RFD "aww shucks," a little Jesus, some stand-up – just not running for anything.

News flash: Agreement that "change" will not include "spare change." Because we're broke, folks! We're putting the 2 trillion dollar war on plastic. We're a wholly owned subsidiary of China/India, Inc. Which is a subsidiary of Halliburton.

But Bush has an economic plan to get us out of the recession. He's negotiated with China to forgive our debt in exchange for three things: (Bill, what are those three things? I'm glad you asked): 1) Mandarin is official language. 2) All white high school grads spend a year in China building railroads and doing laundry. Payback! 3) Naming rights to our country. We choose along with our new President. Choices are, U.S. of Mao. People's Republic of America. Capitalist Running Dog States of America. I like P.R.A. or U.S.M. because it would make for a good chant at the Peking Olympics when the American Chinese team beats the Chinese Chinese team at something – like synchronized spitting.

News flash: someone forgot to lock the nursing home doors! Ralph Nader. 74. RNC hired him to make McCain look young by comparison. Role model for seniors. Never too old to be delusional enough to fuck-up other people's lives (that's 5 "fuck's", Jim. Extra credit!). His campaign slogan is "Unsafe at any age."

News flash: McCain controlled by Commies! POW for 5 years in Vietnam. You've seen the movie, The Manchurian Candidate. Think about McCain. They showed him pictures of Pat Nixon pole dancing in a thong — anybody would crack! So, we elect McCain and some guy in Ho Chi Min city dials up McCain's brain. "Must blow up Blue states." They spare the red states because they think they are fellow communist countries.

Only primary race left is Barack & Hillary. Before Texas and Ohio, I felt sorry for Hillary. Reduced to criticizing his good points: Too eloquent. "Do we want someone answering the red phone in complete sentences? Why start now?" Now it's Barack's lack of experience. He won't be ready on Day

One. Experience at what? "He's never served our country as First Lady. Never greeted a head of State in a yellow pantsuit (...that I've heard of. You'll have to ask him about that....)"

And loyal Bill now says that Hillary wasn't ready on Night One. He rang her phone, and she couldn't answer the call (...don't know if it's true. No direct evidence that Hillary is frigid. Or a lesbian. You'll have to ask her about that....)

Barack has a sex appeal advantage that I think he should exploit. No doubt he'd be ready on Night One. How about an ad: "Hey baby. Sometimes experience does count. Vote for the Black Stud. Oh-oh-oh- Bama!"

COMPARISON OF ELLIE AND BILLY

Contact **(Chapter 1)** Comparison of Ellie and Billy

TIME:

"She turned the dial … and came upon a voice talking excitedly – as far a she could understand, about a Russian machine that was in the sky, endlessly circling the Earth.""

(Sputnik, 1957)

PLACE:

"In her tenth summer, she was taken on vacation to visit two cousins…in the Northern Peninsula of Michigan. Why people who lived on a lake in Wisconsin would spend five hours driving all the way to a Lake in Michigan was beyond her."

(SouthernWisconsin)

TIME QUESTIONS

"Was it possible to travel backwards in time/"

"She found it disquieting that whole blocks of time could be stolen without her knowledge."

"Pi was tied to infinity."

FATHER:

Died of a heart attack when Ellie was in 7th grade

BILLY HORSTMAN:

"No one had ever called Ellie stupid before, and she found herself bursting into tears. Billy Horstman, who sat next to her, gently reached out and placed his hand over hers. His father had recently been indicted for tampering with the odometers on the used cars he sold, so Billy was sensitive to public humiliation. Ellie ran out of the class sobbing."

- doesn't contribute to the plot or to character of Ellie
- never mentioned elsewhere in the novel
- setting back odometers is like going back in time and distance

CONTACT

Carl Sagan spoke to me in August 1985. Sagan was playing the omniscient narrator in his novel *Contact*. I was a passenger in a jet flying east from San Francisco to Chicago. In flight, I began reading the novel.

Contact begins with the childhood of the main character, Ellie Arroway. Ellie lives "on a lake in Wisconsin" in the 1950's. She is still in grade school when her father dies suddenly.

That gets my attention because I, too, lived on a lake (Lake Michigan) in Wisconsin in the 1950's. My father, too, died suddenly when I was in grade school." Weird coincidence. But it gets weirder.

Ellie is now in 7th grade. Her class is studying "pi." She questions her teacher, "How could anybody know that decimals go on and on forever?"

Her teacher responds, "Miss Arroway... this is a stupid question. You're wasting the class's time."

Ellie had never been called stupid before. She bursts into tears. And it's right here on page 11 that Carl Sagan speaks to me. He writes:

Billy Horstman, who sat next to her, gently reached out and placed his hand over hers.

His father had recently been indicted for tampering with the odometers on the used cars that he sold, so Billy was sensitive to public humiliation.

I reread this passage about a dozen times before the plane lands at O'Hare. I reread the earlier passages about Wisconsin, the 1950's, the sudden death of a father.

I think, and have been thinking for the past 32 years, "Holy shit! That's my childhood history and name (Billy). What the fuck are you doing, Carl? (I feel free to call him "Carl" now that he's appropriated chunks of my personal history and, for Christ's sake, my name.)

My gut non-paranoid reaction is that including the 1950's – Wisconsin-sudden death of father– Billy Horstman stuff in a novel must be intentional; that is, it's too many things (4) to be coincidental.

These are details of time, place, and person that do not advance the novel's plot or characters. None of this stuff is mentioned again. It's just very specific information that mirrors my early life that seems to have just been dropped into a much larger and unrelated context, i.e., the whole fucking rest of the novel Contact.

Is this bad proofreading? Did none of the novel's other contributors (including Sagan's wife, Ann Druyan), consultants, editors, or other people (Sagan names 25 in his acknowledgements) who saw the novel before it was published think the Billy Horstman Episode (hereafter the BHE) was odd or without purpose?

Here's a possible paranoid reaction: One or more of the people who had a hand in the novel hatched a plot. And he/she/they are sworn to secrecy – sworn to keep the BHE a mystery forever. Why would they do that? I don't know. I just know there are secret plotters out there trying to mess with me. Fortunately, I don't stray very far down this path.

The alternative to some intent by someone is that the BHE is a coincidence without human, divine, or extraterrestrial intent. Some events fall into patterns that we're just not used to: three grade school classmates from Omaha NE who have lived thousands of miles apart, have not seen nor heard from or about in 50 years run into each other on an elephant safari in Antarctica (fill in any other "improbable" information). No one planned it. It just happened. The classmates are astounded that they have met without planning in such unusual circumstances. 'God moves in mysterious ways," says one; "Must be Fate," says another. "What a baffling coincidence, says the third.

One way of looking at the Antarctic safari is that it had to happen because everything else that ever happened before happened in such a way that the elephant safari couldn't not happen. Everything was set up for that. We don't know why. We've never encountered something so outside our experience or our belief of what can happen. But it happens anyway. Shit happens.

And the BHE? Is the BHE any more remarkable than going to the grocery store? Like the BHE, everything that preceded the grocery trip had to happen exactly as it did. I don't know what animated all those preceding events, but they did happen even if I don't know why they did. Shit happens.

I make some effort to solve the BFE as other than a coincidence or a nefarious plot. I focus on human intent. I look carefully at all the contributors Sagan mentions in his acknowledgments. Anyone there from my old grade school? Anyone who worked with my father, who was chief engineer for a huge steam turbine for Allis Chalmers?

EINSTEIN, NOT ALBERT

Einstein is 24 years old. Not Albert the physicist, but Einstein my son John's cockatiel. The cockatiel Einstein lives in my two bedroom, two-bath condominium in Shorewood, Wisconsin. I used to live there with my son John, but in recent years Einstein is the only full-time resident.

When my wife at the time, Connie, and I bought Einstein as a gift to John for his ninth birthday, we didn't know how long cockatiels could live. We thought it would be somewhere between goldfish and guppies (1week) and dogs and cats (18 years).

We'd had experience with those creatures and blithely assumed that 1 week to 18 years was the established mortality range for all domestic pets except a large parrot or a sea turtle.

It would have been easy enough even in this pre-Google time in human existence (1995) to learn the terminal age of cockatiels (e.g. an encyclopedia, a library, a pet store). But we thought it was common knowledge. No need to research the age question.

We thought our house would be bird-free by the time John was 18. He would be off to college, to a Milwaukee east side rental, or to a South American youth hostel. Maybe Einstein thoughtfully would have used up his allotted years of pet life. And we were right. Sort of. The *house* was bird-free by the time John was 12. By that time, Connie and I were divorced. She was living in what had been "our" house; I was living in my recently acquired condo; John split time between house and condo until he was 18; and Einstein occupied the condo full-time. (You know, typical living arrangements of a 20th Century middleclass American family).

In short, John mostly moved out of both Connie's house and my condo and into an east side Milwaukee house with friends. Einstein stayed not in Connie's house, not in John's flat, but in my condo. One might ask, "Why with me?"

Well, why not? Neither John nor Connie objected to the non-Albert setting up nest in John's condo bedroom. As for me, I like cohabitating with another living being, and Einstein was and still is good company. He has free range of the condo, and he flies from mirror to mirror to admire his image. He puts himself to bed (to nest?) in his cage in John's room each night. He can wolf whistle, say "pretty bird," and "Bill! Bill! Bill" when I come home. He tucks his head under a wing and falls asleep on me when I take a nap or rise in the morning. He picks stray crumbs off my lips and likes to have his head petted.

His presence reminds me of the years when John, Einstein, and I lived together. When John moved to his flat, I stood in his now nearly empty bedroom and watched him walk away and close the condo door. John smiled. "Bye Dad" he said. "See you soon." I waved goodbye from the nearly hollow bedroom, feeling as empty as the room now was.

Einstein satisfies my need to take care of some creature(s). I don't mind the expense to keep Einstein (not Albert) in the home he knows. It doesn't feel like a responsibility.

John is 33, now, I'm 76, Einstein is 24. Only Einstein lives full time by himself in the condo. He gets a visit twice-a-week from John or me. Once, I tried moving him to Evanston IL, where I mostly live now. But he shrieked and paced in his cage and began picking at his feathers whenever I left him alone. He wanted to come home.

He leads a simple life. No existential questions. Food and water show up every 3 days along with the two people he knows best. He has at least one mirror in each room to peck and talk to. It's a quiet, orderly, predictable life. In this way, he reminds me of Garrison Keillor's Norwegian bachelor farmers.

So, Einstein, I say "Uff da" to you. Hang in there a good while longer. If you die before I do, I'll miss you greatly, If I go first, you will at last get to live full time with your other surrogate parent -- a once-nine-year-old boy named John.

Bill Horstman
April 23, 2020

FLY ROD: IMAGINING MY FATHER

(November 2017 draft)
(June 2019) draft

This story began with a book. The book led me to a fly fishing rod. I'd like to say the fly rod led me to a trout. But it's late November in Wisconsin and the trout have gone deep and still in their pools.

The book is *Casting a Spell: the Bamboo Fly Rod and the American Pursuit of Perfection* by George Black. What the book began is a memory of my father and of a fly fishing rod he made 70 years ago.

My father was an engineer and a craftsman and a fisherman. He was born on a southern Indiana farm in the last year of the 19th century, the oldest surviving child of seven. He was named Elmer, a popular name in that time and place but now in long disuse. As a boy, he fished with makeshift rods and cane poles on Hough Creek, which wended along the border of his family's farm, and on the nearby White River into which Hough Creek flowed and still flows. Catfish, crappies, bluegills, and bass.

He was good at making useful things from the materials at hand, mostly wood. Barn stalls for the cows. Kitchen chairs. Bed frames and dressers for his three younger brothers and one sister. Rifle stocks. And poles for fishing. One piece poles eight to ten feet long with a sturdy spine to flip fat bass onshore; poles that taper to a tip that twitches at the slightest nibble of fish lips on night crawler.

My father graduated from Brownstown High School in 1918 as class valedictorian. America had entered WWI - the Great War, the war to end all wars - and nativistic anti-German sentiment was strong. Strong enough in Indiana, where the Governor was a member of the KKK, that my father – who was the grandson of German immigrants and who attended a German-speaking Lutheran church - was denied the scholarship that traditionally went to the high school valedictorian.

Even without the scholarship, my father had saved enough from local farm work to attend Purdue University. Though he had been financially penalized because of his German heritage, he enlisted in the U.S. Army R.O.T.C. at Purdue. A young German-American man preparing to fight young German-German men. He graduated in 1923 with a degree in mechanical engineering. Still designing and creating things. More complicated things – engines, machine components, and city block-long steam turbines - things made from steel.

But the natural world and its materials still held him. He had a workshop in the basement of our 1940s Milwaukee home that was tool heaven: a lathe, a vise, jig saw, table saw, router, chisels, calipers, a soldering iron, blowtorch, ball peen and claw hammers, drills, a level, an angle, planes and punches, screws and nails — and wood. Lots of wood. Walnut. Maple. Oak. Ash. Pine. Hickory and Butternut.

Weekdays after dinner, my two sisters and I would follow our father into this wonderland of exotic tools and wood of many grains and hues. We were allowed to use small hand tools to saw at rough lumber, to pound nails and drill holes in scraps of wood. We made un-designed, mutant objects that we took upstairs at bedtime and proudly displayed on our dressers.

While we slept, our father made objects of beauty and utility. A graceful, curved walnut chair with a cane seat for each of his three children. He made an armoire, a dresser, and a bed with pears and apples carved on the headboard for his wife. For himself, he made fishing rods. Bait casting rods. And fly rods of split bamboo.

He made the fly fishing rod of this story in 1946, home from a year-long Army tour rebuilding power plants in post-WW II Germany. He was forty-seven and I was two. He would live five more years. Though he's been gone since 1951, I'm looking at his fly rod right now. It was in a storage locker, nearly forgotten in the flotsam of my parents' lives.

The shaft of this fly rod is made of Tonkin cane, which, as George Black's book explains, is bamboo from China's Guangdong Province. Before Mao Tse Tung's revolutionary forces gained control of mainland China in 1949,

Tonkin cane was exported to the United States and other western countries and used to make fly rods that were prized for their unmatched combination of strength and suppleness.

My father's fly rod is in three sections joined to each other by ferrules of nickel silver. The shaft tapers elegantly from one-half inch diameter where it abuts the cork grip to one-eighth inch at the tip. Four snake guides to hold the fishing line remain, wrapped to the shaft by red silk thread and sealed in varnish. One snake guide and the top guide are gone, their absence marked by silk shreds and small patches of bare bamboo. Pits left by hooks mark the cork grip. On the shaft, an inch from the grip, in precise script, beneath age-ambered varnish, the India ink states: *Aug 1946*.

What is a man of 70 (me) to do with such a discovery? Is there another story that I might shape that taps meaning from this story of chance convergence of a book, an artifact, and a memory.

An appealing public story might end by telling how the fly rod was rebuilt, how the grown son stood midstream in waders and landed a brook trout, how the rod became a living touchstone between father and son. But I can't in truth tell that story. I'm not the craftsman or the fisherman that my father was. I can't reconstruct the fly rod or use it with his skill.

Writing about the fly rod, now able to appreciate its material and artistry, has let me re-imagine my father's character and creativity, parts of him that I as an eight year old didn't see when he was alive.

People connect through what they create. People are born. People die. In between time, they make things - a fly rod, engines, chairs, friendships, a family, wounds, wars, stories.

People are born. People die. Long after their bodies have separated into atoms and dispersed through the Universe, their creations continue to connect them to the living world. It's an elemental, everyday story. Creation. Connection. Everyone can tell versions of it.

One of mine begins this way: "This story began with a book. The book led to a fly-fishing rod. I'd like to say the fly rod led me to a trout. But it's late November in Wisconsin and the trout have gone deep and still in their pools."

Bill Horstman
December 2013
Revised November 2017
Photos:

Purdue ROTC uniform head shot
North Freedom with bait casting rod
Elmer/Zel sitting back to back
Formal photo
Children's chair
WWII Germany in uniform
Standing with engineers in front of steam turbine
Indiana family photo with 3 kids
Tosa home
Fly rod with Aug 1946 inscription

HIGH SCHOOL

1957 vs. 2010

Scenario 1:
Jack goes quail hunting before school and then pulls into the school parking lot with his shotgun in his truck's gun rack.
1957 - Vice Principal comes over, looks at Jack's shotgun, goes to his car, and gets his shotgun to show Jack.
2010 - School goes into lock down, FBI called, Jack hauled off to jail and never sees his truck or gun again. Counselors called in for traumatized students and teachers.

Scenario 2:
Johnny and Mark get into a fist fight after school.
1957 - Crowd gathers. Mark wins. Johnny and Mark shake hands and end up buddies.
2010 - Police called and SWAT team arrives — they arrest both Johnny and Mark. They are both charged with assault and both expelled even though Johnny started it.

Scenario 3:
Jeffrey will not be still in class, he disrupts other students.
1957 - Jeffrey sent to the Principal's office and given a good paddling by the Principal. He then returns to class, sits still and does not disrupt class again.
2010 - Jeffrey is given huge doses of Ritalin. He becomes a zombie. He is then tested for ADD. The family gets extra money (SSI) from the government because Jeffrey has a disability.

Scenario 4:

Billy breaks a window in his neighbor's car, and his Dad gives him a whipping with his belt.
1957 - Billy is more careful next time, grows up normal, goes to college and becomes a successful businessman.
2010 - Billy's dad is arrested for child abuse, Billy is removed to foster care

and joins a gang. The state psychologist is told by Billy's sister that she remembers being abused herself, and their dad goes to prison. Billy's mom has an affair with the psychologist.

Scenario 5:
Mark gets a headache and takes some aspirin to school.
1957 - Mark shares his aspirin with the Principal out on the smoking dock.
2010 - The police are called and Mark is expelled from school for drug violations. His car is then searched for drugs and weapons.

Scenario 6:
Pedro fails high school English.
1957 - Pedro goes to summer school, passes English and goes to college.
2010 - Pedro's cause is taken up by state. Newspaper articles appear nationally explaining that teaching English as a requirement for graduation is racist. ACLU files class action lawsuit against the state school system and Pedro's English teacher. English is then banned from core curriculum. Pedro is given his diploma anyway but ends up mowing lawns for a living because he cannot speak English.

Scenario 7:
Johnny takes apart leftover firecrackers from the Fourth of July, puts them in a model airplane paint bottle and blows up a red ant bed.
1957 - Ants die.
2010 - ATF, Homeland Security and the FBI are all called. Johnny is charged with domestic terrorism. The FBI investigates his parents - and all siblings are removed from their home and all computers are confiscated. Johnny's dad is placed on a terror watch list and is never allowed to fly again.

Scenario 8:
Johnny falls while running during recess and scrapes his knee. He is found crying by his teacher, Mary. Mary hugs him to comfort him.
1957 – In a short time, Johnny feels better and goes on playing.
2010 - Mary is accused of being a sexual predator and loses her job. She faces 3 years in State Prison. Johnny undergoes 5 years of therapy.

HIGHLIGHT OF FIG'S SUMMER

He captured a cicada in his mouth. Didn't chew it. Didn't swallow it. Carried it, buzzing furiously, in his mouth for several blocks before it escaped.

The next day, he nosed up to another cicada (or maybe it was his old cicada who had escaped), and we said, "Oh look, he's going to capture another cicada." Indeed, Fig captures this cicada in his mouth. This time, it is followed by a loud crunch. No more buzzing.

Lesson: Cicadas make shitty pets.

Bill & Fig look- alikes at dog park, Evanston IL summer 2015

Bill & mother Rosella (Zel) Lieder Horstman, Wauwatosa WI 1971

Bill as Dudley Do-Right for Halloween at
ancestral home, N. Freedom WI 2006

Bill at Bike the Drive, Chicago IL 5.28.2017

Bill at Harry's Bar, Rome, Italy 5.6.2018

Bill finding Morel mushrooms at cottage (former
chicken coop), N. Freedom WI 5.20.2006

Bill relaxing with Saki & Fig in office, Evanston IL 1.4.2011

Bill's dad Elmer Horstman, Brownstown IN 1929

Bill's retirement at UWM, Shorewood WI 5.10.2007

Sally & Bill at St. Mark's Sq. Venice, Italy May 2018

"JOKES" ROUTINE

Traditional "stand-up" comics mostly used to tell jokes. Guys like Rodney Dangerfield. Buddy Hackett. Henny Youngman. They'd throw out these snappy one-liners so fast that once you started to laugh, you never had enough time to recover before the next joke hit you. (Tell 3-4 one-liners). Their shtick was to get you in these laughing-jags where you couldn't catch your breath and your sides hurt, and you'd be yelling, "Stop, stop, I'm dying here." But they wouldn't stop.

For our parents' generation, this was considered "fun." You'd eat a big meal in a club or at a Las Vegas show, drink hard liquor, and laugh like crazy at the comedian's jokes until a chunk of prime rib got stuck in your windpipe; the bouncer would perform the Heimlich maneuver on you; or the Maître' D would call the Coroner; and the show would be over. For you anyway. And for your sister Sylvia, who inhaled a plate of shrimp scampi.

But now, jokes are what people send on email. At least at the office, it's the main purpose of email. Your company sends notices that email is to be used only for business purposes. But they just don't know. I mean, it is POSSIBLE to use your company's email for work — it CAN be used for business purposes. But it isn't. It's really just there to send jokes.

These days comedians who perform have a "routine." They project a *character,* a *persona* who has a quirky *outlook* on one or more of the following nine topics – men, women, sex, politics, celebrities, sex, current news, people from other countries, and sex – those nine topics. And tell *stories* with smart-ass commentary.

Well, I don't have a routine tonight. I was pressed into this slot at the last minute, subbing for a pair of juggling Chihuahuas ... just before the show, it was discovered that their immigration documents were phony. So, I'm just going to tell a few jokes. That should be okay though – jokes are something solid that you can take with you when you leave here tonight and that, when you get to work on Monday, you can send out on email.

The particular kind of joke I'm going to tell is what you might call a "dumb person" joke. These are jokes that are aimed at some group of people that you and your friends like to think of as being dumber than you are. This kind of joke is so common that you have to think that it must have existed in all times and all places.

There probably was a Neanderthal who amused his knuckle dragging friends: "Did you hear about the Cro-Magnon who asked his wife to cook a wooly mammoth, but they didn't have fire yet?" The Neanderthals were not skilled humorists, and thankfully they died out (or were killed by their audiences) and we have been spared listening to their jokes. Except, sadly for us, this one that was found by archaeologists on a cave wall in France – signed by its author, Francois, with a charred stick. Although the archaeologists were smart enough to decipher the pictographs and translate them into modern languages, they also were tasteless and uncaring enough to preserve this joke, which is terrible even by Neanderthal standards. So, "thanks" archaeologists (say "faux brightly")!

I'm sure, too, there is a guy in Baghdad right now saying to his Kurdish buddies, "Hey, did you hear about the Sunni suicide bomber who went into a Shiite mosque but forgot to connect the detonating device? He pushes the button to send himself straight to paradise and nothing happens. Well the Mullah sees him and says...." (pause) Hell, I don't know the punch line to this guy's joke. I'm from Milwaukee. I think mosques are what kids wear over their faces at Halloween. But you get the idea. People are very tribal and territorial about their "dumb people" jokes.

When I was growing up in Milwaukee in the 1950s, the "dumb people" we told jokes about were people of Polish descent – "Polacks." We made fun of their last names (Polish eye exam joke). We made fun of their language (3 Polish cowboys joke). And we made fun of their purported simple-mindedness (find a joke). These are not great jokes, but remember, we were nine years old.

We also told jokes about all kinds of people who weren't "us" — Catholics, Jews, Nee-grows, country folks, southerners, teachers, what we called "morons,"(generic dumb people), kids who went to a different grade school — basically anyone who didn't live on our block.

I guess we were not very nice. But as far as I could tell, neither were the kids we told jokes about. I'd be crossing 68th street, telling a friend a joke about the dumb kids on the next block. And as soon as we got to the other side of the median, a bunch of kids from the next block would run up to us, yell, "Hey, you, stupid," and beat us up.

On one side of the middle of the street, we were smart and safe. One foot away, we were stupid and brutalized. Smart-stupid, smart-stupid (hop from one foot to the other). It was like a field trip for a bi-polar school– not a school for bi-polar kids, but a regular school like all the others — that takes normal children and fucks them up. I went to a school that trained kids to be clinically depressed. Every day before class, all the children would report to the school nurse, Frau Himmler, who would poke needles in our skulls and extract serotonin.

These days, the most popular "dumb people" are not Polish immigrants but… what do you call those people with real light hair — blondes, right. (tell 2 quick blond jokes).

Before telling my *favorite* blonde joke, I want to tell you this true story about my friends Kurt and Tiffany. Recently, Kurt, who was born in Germany, found out that one of Tiffany's grandmothers is Polish. Which by the rules of bigotry makes Tiffany Polish, too — you know, "all you need is one drop of Polish blood." Kurt (that swine) says he knows it's true — that Tiffany really is Polish — by how quickly she surrendered to a German.

Tiffany is – by the American-Bimbo standard – a very pretty woman: large, electric blue eyes, big mane of blond hair, and (you know) — boobs. And like all certifiably beautiful females, when she's driving a car, she speeds. She knows that if she gets pulled over, the chances still are very high that the cop will be a man, that even in the age of "Brokeback" he's likely to be straight, and that she'll get a warning and not a ticket. She likes this game. It's like going to Pottawatomie only the odds are much better. So she drives FAST.

One day, Tiffany is speeding along and she gets pulled over by a cop. Only this cop is a woman. And she's a blond. Tiffany is freaked. She knows she was doing 90. She knows that the boobs, the eyes, the hair are useless to her—unless the blond lady cop is gay. But Tif doesn't want to play that game – probably thinking her Polish, very Catholic grandmother's ghost would put a curse on her.

Anyway, the cop says, "Your driver's license, please."

Tiffany, without the use of her usual tools, can't think straight and starts rummaging around in her purse. She's never had to produce a driver's license before and has forgotten what it looks like. "Um, what does the license look like?" she asks the officer.

"It's small, rectangle shape, and it's got your picture on it," says the cop.

Tiffany finds a small, rectangular object in her purse. It's a make-up mirror. She looks in it, sees her face, and says, "Oh, here it is!" Hands it to the officer.

The blond officer takes the mirror, looks in it, hands it back and says, "Sorry, you can go. I didn't know you were a cop, too."

Ha! I don't have another blond joke that's my favorite. THAT was my favorite blond joke: It's got not one, but two, dumb blonds in it. And a Polack. And a Kraut. And fast cars. And cops. And I got to lie – it's not a true story. For a kid who grew up (I didn't say matured") in Milwaukee in the 1950s — that is as good as it gets.

May 2006

LETTER TO FAMILY 2018
(WITH HELP FROM SALLY)

Dear family and friends,

We wish each of you good health, progress toward achieving your life goals, and a peace of spirit too seldom found in our world.

Bill and Sally had a well-traveled year. In February, Sally made a now annual ski trip to Vail to visit her NU sophomore roommate, Barb. In May, we spent three weeks traversing Italy by train, bus, auto, boat and our feet. We spent over a week in Rome absorbing the treasures of ancient art and architecture, watching the Italian Tennis Open and consuming excellent food, wine, cappuccino and especially gelato.

From Rome, we went by high speed train to Venice and then Milan. We rented a car and drove to a Florentine villa, staying on the way in Rapallo and hiking to two seaside villages of the Cinque Terre. And, of course, we had to visit Pisa and walk the ancient wall of Lucca. Finally, we ferried to the island of Capri, staying in the land of lemons for several days before capping our trip with a drive up the Amalfi coast. Throughout Italy, people were uniformly gracious and welcoming to us.

After returning from Italy, Sally gave notice to her employer of 3-1/2 years and became a consultant to her former employer plus two other companies. During a December business trip to Cabo San Lucas, Sally was joined by her daughter Michelle for a mother-daughter weekend.

In August, we drove to Santa Fe for the annual Indian Market and then to Taos for sunshine, tennis, music and friends. Northern New Mexico is one of our favorite destinations. It's a happy mix of cultures, spectacular scenery and vibrant outdoor life.

Sally's family (son Jesse and daughter Michelle) continue to live in the Chicago area. Michelle has a relationship with a very nice man named Luke. They live in the Chicago condominium that Michelle purchased three years ago.

Bill's four kids (Missy, Matt, Andy and John), three grandkids (Madison, Alex and Ryan), daughter-in-law (Diane) and son-in-law (Jack) continue to live, work, study and play in southeastern Wisconsin. Madison (Maddy) is a 17 year old high school senior and has just been accepted into the nursing program at UW-Oshkosh.

We are fortunate to live close enough to our families to stay involved in each other's lives.

Again, we wish you a safe and fulfilling 2019.

LETTER TO MADDY FOR COMMUNION 2018

Dear Maddy,

As you prepare for Communion this year, I want you to know (I hope you already do know) that I'm very proud of you both for your accomplishments and for the kind of person you have become. And, of course, that I love you.

I remember my own preparation for Communion nearly 60 years ago at Mt Olive Lutheran Church in Wauwatosa. I probably was NOT an ideal communicant in the eyes of my church; that is, although outwardly I conformed and went through the process of study leading to Confirmation, inwardly I questioned and thought about everything that was taught.

Looking back, this was a good thing because it strengthened the beliefs and values I've carried through my life. At least for me, doubt and questioning, thinking and discussion have been needed steps to help make my beliefs and values my own. It's an approach to a mature spiritual life that I highly recommend.

You are a remarkable person, a woman who will stumble on occasion (as we all do), but who will pick herself up again. I see in you kindness, care for others, perseverance, intelligence, and a will to create – qualities embodied by Jesus.

Best wishes and love from me to you in your spiritual quest.

Much love,
Pops

MOVIES I'VE WATCHED AT LEAST 5 TIMES

The Godfather
Godfather II
Annie Hall
Love and Death
Manhattan
Sleeper
The Way We Were
Blazing Saddles
Young Frankenstein
The Princess Bride

2001: A Space Odyssey
Dr. Strangelove
Casablanca
The Maltese Falcon
Philadelphia Story
Groundhog Day
Chinatown
Life of Brian
Charade
When Harry Met Sally

Singin' In the Rain
Holiday Inn
Wallace & Gromit: Three Amazing Adventures
Indiana Jones
Indiana Jones and the Last Crusade
A Christmas Carol (with Alistar Sim)
Star Wars (1-3)
The Shining

A Fish Called Wanda
High Fidelity
Dogma
Saving Private Ryan
Peter Pan
Animal House
Goldfinger
Dr. No
A Room With A View
Lawrence of Arabia

The Shawshank Redemption

The Prime of Miss Jean Brodie
Dr. Zhivago
Moonrise Kingdom
Gone With the Wind
The Wizard of Oz
Meet Me In St. Louis
Men In Black
Field of Dreams
It Happened One Night

UHF

NEWBORN

clapped hands and whistles
cannot undream my son

sound and stillness
play him a seamless tune

far from my terror
of his untouched sleep

OF MICE & ME

Part I: Mice

The first mouse appeared on Wednesday morning August 5. Sally and I were in the kitchen hunched over cups of coffee. I looked up and saw our cat, Saki, staring at a badly bitten but still breathing mouse lying in front of the refrigerator. I picked up the mouse, carried it to our dumpster in the alley and dropped it still alive into the garbage.

That's how it began. Of course, we didn't know it was a beginning, didn't know that dumpster mouse was the first of 33 Saki and I would kill over the next 28 days. It was just one mouse, after all. And it wasn't the first dead or wounded mouse Saki had dragged into the kitchen for us to admire together, to share some quality time. This new mouse was nothing too unusual.

In the past, when a new dead mouse appeared, we would find a scattering of mouse scat in the cabinet under the kitchen sink. Water pipes extend through the cabinet from the sink to the basement via a hole in the floor just large enough to accommodate a hot water pipe, a cold water pipe and a mouse.

Or mice as we learned on Thursday morning August 6. That morning, a second mouse, this one fully dead, lay on the kitchen floor. Saki sat over it, twitching her tail, looking at it with sociopathic calm.

"Two mice in two days," Sally said. "I don't like this. Do you think there might be mouse poop in the cabinet under the sink?" This, I knew, was not really a question.

So I dropped dead mouse number two in the dumpster next to now-dead mouse number one. Then I wedged my head and one hand into the under-sink cabinet, small flashlight held between my teeth, and emptied the cabinet of pans, Tupperware containers, detergent bottles, a cast iron hamburger flattener, steel wool … and lots of mouse scat.

"Hmmm," Sally said, " do you think we should put a trap in the cabinet tonight in case there's a third mouse?" She reached in the drawer under the butcher-block counter and pulled out a mousetrap. "Let's do it," Sally said and handed the trap to me.

The trap design was simple: a spring with a metal bar was attached to a 2" by 4" wood base. When a mouse nudged a trip lever, the spring would instantly release, and the metal bar would smash onto the mouse. On its wood base, the trap had the word VICTOR writ large. Larger still, was a blood red letter V and the outline of a mouse head.

Thursday night, I put VICTOR in the cabinet, its bar in the armed position, its trip lever loaded with Aldi's Peanut Delight crunchy peanut butter, an irresistible mélange of peanut pieces, sugar, salt, molasses, hydrogenated vegetable oil and very low price.

Friday morning August 7. No dead mouse lay on the kitchen floor. But Saki had her nose to the door of the under-sink cabinet. In the cabinet was a mousetrap with a mouse attached to it, its head crushed by the metal bar. "Three in three days, " Sally said. "Do you think there might be more?"

I took dead mouse number three to the dumpster, pulled the spring bar up, and shook the mouse off VICTOR and into eternity. I stood in the alley and Goggled mouse reproduction on my smartphone. Google told me that one family of mice in a single location could increase from 6 to 60 in three months and sustain that size. We definitely had a problem. Later Friday, I followed the kitchen water pipes into the basement. A hole led between the basement walls where a brick had fallen out: nice mice territory. I bought another VICTOR trap and that night put it, loaded with delicious Aldi Peanut Delight, in the under-sink cabinet and put another trap near the hole in the basement wall.

Saturday morning August 8. A dead mouse in each trap. Five mice in four days. I set two more traps.

Also on Saturday, I started a ledger to record how many mice Saki and I killed each day. The ledger had a box that I drew near its top with the words,

MICE (unknown number), in it. Every morning, I made a pencil mark for each mouse that Saki or I had killed since the previous morning. The ledger stayed on our kitchen counter from Saturday August 8 to Wednesday September 2. It was a teutonically neat and orderly Scorecard of Death.

Over the next 26 days, Saki got fewer and fewer mice, and my traps got more and more. She was like John Henry against the steam-powered hammer, working as hard as she could but losing, losing to the forces of mechanization.

The number of mice killed reached a climax between August 20 and 25 when 12 mice were killed, bringing the total to 31. Abruptly, no more mice. A week passed. No mice.

But it was not quite over. On September 2, a large mouse, 5 inches from nose to tail end, was caught in the cabinet trap, which it had dragged across the floor. Not a quick or painless death. The next day, a very small mouse no longer than my thumb from tip to first knuckle was pinned in the basement trap, its head nearly severed. Then it was over. Finally.

Part II: Me

Although I had kept setting traps, any satisfaction I initially took in mouse trapping and death documenting was long gone. The Scorecard of Death now felt creepy. Was I trying to reduce each mangled mouse into a pencil mark on a sheet of paper? Was I trying to make a way for me to look away from the killing? If so, it hadn't worked. I had seen too many crushed skulls, snapped spines and sightless eyes to believe that my dead mice were pencil marks in some counting game. It was not a game. Just an ugly job.

I learned a lot about mice in 29 days: what they like to eat, where they like to live, their rate of reproduction, their family life, their many predators. How close they live every day to the edge between life and death. I also learned that mice are enough like humans that I empathize with them: they have one head, on which are two eyes, two ears, one mouth and one nose; they are warm blooded, industrious, family oriented, and peanut butter loving. Like us, they feel fear and pain. They are aware.

I see mice in my house as pests. They eat stored food and can carry disease and lice; they chew books and blankets for their nests and dispense turds in my cupboards. From this point of view, it makes sense to get them out of the house, to kill them if need be.

But in killing this family of mice, in watching them die one-by-one, day-by-bloody-day, I have come to see them as more than pests, more than just a nuisance to be gotten rid of. To my discomfort, I came to see the mice as fellow creatures trying, like us, to live their lives with what the cosmos had given them. We happened to have been born as humans; they happened to have been born as mice.

September 2015 (33 Mice)
Revised June, 2019 (Of Mice & Me)

THE NORMAL DAILY ROUTINE FOR FIG, SAKI, AND RC: AUGUST 2016

- Fig gets out 2-3 times daily - morning (before 10:00), dinnertime (4:30 – 6:30), and evening (9:00– midnight). Melinda will do Fig's morning and dinnertime walk/run and the feeding for Fig & Saki and RC at the same time. Fig normally has 2 bowel movements each day (morning & night).

- If it's wet or muddy, please wipe Fig's paws (rag/towel inside back door) when he comes in.

- Fig gets fed in the morning and early evening: 1/3 can wet dog food and a handful (maybe a cup) of dry food, mix of Science Diet and Bill Jack (above the washer/dryer next to the back door) each time. Change the water daily in his bowl in the kitchen. He can get some treats (on same shelf as canned dog food).

- Saki gets fed on top of the counter by the window in the kitchen at the same 2 times that Fig does. 3/4 small can wet cat food each meal. She can also have a bit of dry food.

- Saki should stay inside. If the weather is nice, she will try to slip out the door when you enter or leave. She has her litter box, water bowl, and sleeping cushion in the upstairs bathroom. Check her litter box for poop each day & deposit it in the toilet. A scoop is behind the litter box. Extra litter is in the small linen closet next to the upstairs bathroom.

- RC needs his food & water (small yellow hanging trays inside his cage) checked each day. He gets a mix of the plain pellets, the colored pellets, and a bit of broken-up Avi cake (food packages above washer/dryer).

- Cover his cage at night with the 2 covers that are next to the cage. RC can have his cage door open during the day only. During the day, hang covers over back of cage

- Note: Small black ants have invaded the kitchen & are attracted to ANY exposed food. Ant traps are placed all over the kitchen, so the ants will soon start disappearing.

PLAGUE TALK

SHELTERING IN PLACE
NEW NORMAL
SOCIAL DISTANCING
VIRUS
CONTAGIOUS
COVID 19
CORONAVIRUS
FLATTENING THE CURVE
MITIGATE
ROLLING RE-ENTRY
HUNKER DOWN
FRONT LINES
HEROES
1ST RESPONDERS
PANDEMIC
TOGETHER
ISOLATION
TESTING
EPICENTER
QUARANTINE
ASYMPTOMATIC
SPREAD
RE-OPEN
EPIDEMIOLOGY
TIMES (TRYING,UNCERTAIN,DIFFICULT,CHALLENGING THESE)
P95 FACE MASK
SURGICAL FACE MASK
COMMUNITY TRANSMISSION
FAUCI
STAY AT HOME
SECOND WAVE
SUPPLY CHAIN
VENTILATOR

2020

ROSES ARE RED

Roses are red,
platypuses are indeterminate.

You're the cutest
human girl in the friggin' firmament.

A Late-Friday Poem for You
[Received May 9, 2008]

SIX POEMS

City Wind

wind today

trees creak
snow & trash fly

the lake looks
psychotic

a leather jacket
is my shelter

18

my hook
in moving air
that held

untethered boy
flying now
in new wind

I watch
below
becalmed

Afternoon In the Park

it must be October
or maybe November
who knows

pale sun
leaches color
an old photograph

the footpath
is deserted
except for leaves

and old men
losing their minds

Escher's Dogs

beneath the tail
of doggie one

grows the nose
of doggie two

whose tail in turn
sprouts the snout

of doggie three
repeat that now

eternally

Shadow

I am the shadow of an incorporeal man
you conceived immaculate and nurture alone
planning for my birth

Jasper

the skier moved softly
through dark snow

unaware of the dog

dying nearby
beside the tracks

SLEET

Sleet. Two inches and counting. Fig wants a walk or, better yet, a run.

I find my North Face hooded parka, insulated gloves, alpaca knit cap, lined jeans, wool socks, neck gaiter, Sorel boots, and a scarf to bind them all.

Then it's Fig's turn. Wraparound, red and gray body coat, Vaseline between his toes to prevent ice-balls, a harness, and a leash to bind them all. We are ready!

Quick three block walk to a small park. Fig sprints around, pees on everything higher than 3 inches, rolls in the sleet, snorts and puffs, and at one point just barks into the 30+ mph wind. I lumber after him, assaulted by cheek-stinging sleet, thinking of the hot black tea and Christmas colored Hershey's Kisses waiting back at the house.

After 10 minutes in the park, Fig has eliminated from his body all that can be. He settles down on a patch of windswept grass and chews a stick.

Time to go. Fig agrees to let me put his leash back on but insists on carrying his new friend, the stick, back to the house where he drops it for future use on the now buried back porch. Sleet.

January 2017

STILL LIFE FOR DUNKIN

Day is here. Finally. He's still gone.

Wake with Bob Marley's "Redemption Song" playing in my head.

Cat's collar-bell rings in the hallway. She's searching.

Gather his white fur from bathroom waste basket. Make a fur-ball
for my desk.

Sunny. Like yesterday, day zero.

Walk to get coffee and the *Trib*. Usual route – up the alley with dog-edible
garbage scraps; to the fire hydrant at the corner; on the grass to cedar trees
in Eiden Park; east into the sun on Main Street.

Guy on the sidewalk selling *Streetwise* asks, Hey, where's your dog?" I tell
him what happened. "Sorry, man."

Does everyone walking here have a dog? It looks that way this morning. I
follow a man with a Husky that looks like Dunkin. A ghost?

Think of the expression, "I'll be doggoned." That's me. Dog gone.

Tuck an empty poop-scoop bag in my shirt pocket today.

Nearing home. Muddy tennis balls, rubber bone, duct-taped cuddle-toys,
ragged blanket piled around the front porch planter. A memorial and a notice
by Sally. Death here today. I add a *Pooch Park* Frisbee.

Yolanta quietly cleans the house. Our parrot, RC, screams "Dunkin!" when
she nears his cage.

Jildou of the Dutch family next door sits on their deck and pours imaginary tea. Dressed as always in pink and lavender.

Will time pass quickly again? I guess so. But not yet. Not this morning.

June 2019

SUMMER WITH CICADAS SINGING

Cicadas began buzzing
in our big elms
sooner than most years

their song marking both
high summer and
a tilt toward fall

The promise of coming loss
hints of nostalgia
enter our bright days

and like midlife
we see shadows now
in the light

SYNCHRONICITY: A TRUE TOOTH STORY

My son, John, was 5 years old and in kindergarten at the UWM Child Care Center. One early November day, John's class was jumping in leaf piles beneath the oak trees at the edge of the Downer Woods. It was overcast and windy and leaves were swirling.

Following a lunchtime workout at the nearby Klotsche Center, I was walking toward my office in Holton Hall. I looked to my right and saw the group of kids with their teachers. One kid appeared to be crying. His jacket looked familiar, so I walked over to the group. The crying kid was John.

John said that he was playing in the leaf piles when Nathan jumped on him and knocked out his tooth - his first loose tooth. The teachers and kids all had been looking for the tooth beneath the blowing piles of leaves, and now they had to return to the Child Care Center.

I asked John if he remembered where he was when the tooth came out. He pointed in the direction of the leaves and trees. "Somewhere over there," he said, indicating the entire length of the woods' edge.

Thinking only that it might be easier for John to leave holding a bit of hope, I said that I'd stay and continue to look for his tooth.

The children and their teachers began walking away. John waved good-by. I walked directly to a randomly chosen leaf pile, crouched down, brushed leaves away in one spot, and looked at the gravel covered ground. Instantly, I looked at one piece of material, picked it up ... and it was a tooth.

"John," I shouted toward the group that was now near Chapman Hall, "I found your tooth!"

The group stopped. I walked to them and gave John his tooth.

Now, years later, I wonder if the five-year-old children thought this was normal, was the kind of thing that all their parents could just do. I think all the adults, including me, felt we had been brushed by magic.

1992
Shared July 17, 2010

THE BIG MELT

Yesterday's clean white
snow mountains
have morphed today to
gritty ponds of water and ice

strewn with
lost mittens, dirt
and dog goop
a pretty low score
on the aesthetics-o- meter
but do not grieve
for when there's
slush and grime,
can Spring be
far behind?

February 28, 2021

TOSA '61 REUNION QUIZ

1. Name five Gilles' specialty sundaes?

2. What Tosa teacher ran the 1,500 meter race on the 1948 U.S. Olympic team?

3. How many classmates watched an entire movie at the Bluemound Drive-In?

4. What was Miss (Gladys) Garness's underground nickname (at least with the boys)?

5. What popular novel had the most underlined passages and earmarked pages?

6. What were the other high schools in the 1960-61 Suburban Conference?

7. What was the popular chemical product used to simulate a suntan?

8. How many Red Allow girls kept their pledges of non-smoking and non-drinking during their high school years?

9. How many by the end of June 1962?

10. What Olympic sports (but high school non-varsity and non-club sports) did Mr. Pacetti teach after school in the basement?

11. Couples drove to the Lakefront on weekend nights to watch the races of what naval craft?

12. What the hell is a HEEMEA?

13. When boys cruised Wisconsin Avenue at night, for what kind of bird were they looking?

14. What restaurant had the most butter dripping from its garlic bread?

15. What was the name of the "beatnik" coffee house on E. North Ave (near Frenchy's Restaurant and the Oriental Theater)?

16. What were the names of the drug store, the dry goods store, and the ice cream & candy store in the Tosa village?

17. In the movie Summer Place, what condition did Sandra Dee's condition get in?

18. What is the theme song from Breakfast at Tiffany's?

19. James Dean, Natalie Wood, and Sal Mineo starred in Rebel Without a Cause. But what actor who later became a counterculture star had a bit role in the movie?

20. What caused classmates to say "padiddle" & what happened when it was said?

21. Who was "Miss V" and how was her surname spelled?

22. Who was John Kasdorf's main competition for best running back in the Suburban Conference?

23. In 1961 Milwaukee, what did the following words have in common? — Bluemound, Broadway, Glenview, Greenfield, Spring, Uptown

24. In 1960, Detroit's "Big Three" automakers introduced what 3 "compact" cars?

25. What manufactured-in-Kenosha car had an infamous fold-down back seat?

26. Did Wauwatosa vote Republican or Democrat in the 1960 Presidential election?

27. How could you tell what Mr. (Caesar) Street had for breakfast?

28. Who said, "Just the facts, M'am"? (Name the character, actor, and TV show)

29. In October 1960, Nikita Khrushchev used his shoe to pound his desk at the United Nations. What brand of shoe did he use?

30. Why did the music die on February 3, 1959?

TWO LIMERICKS IN HONOR OF ERIKA SANDER ON THE OCCASION OF HER INDUCTION AS EMERITA INTO THE UWM HR DEPARTMENT - AUGMENTED

There was a woman named Erika
who knew how to drink and swearika

one day at a lunch
she o'er spiked her punch

now she's god-knows whereika.

There was a Prof named Sander
whose admin skills did land her

in charge of HR
where both near and far

she spoke with startling candor.

August 28, 2008

WHEN YOU DIE

all your atoms
decide to
stop organizing
with you
as their purpose

where you are
and who is
with you
or not
doesn't matter

they just agree
you're too much trouble
and head off
to the basement
or Jupiter

every some trillion
eons or every
millisecond
all your old atoms
run into each other

on a random street corner
and decide to play
you again
precisely like
the times before

May 2020

Printed in the United States
by Baker & Taylor Publisher Services

Printed in the United States
by Baker & Taylor Publisher Services